FAMILY MATTERS

You and a Death in Your Family

Antoine Wilson

the rosen publishing group's
rosen
central

For Eric Wilson and Jason Harman, two brilliant and creative individuals who left us too soon.

Published in 2001 by The Rosen Publishing Group, Inc.
29 East 21st Street, New York, NY 10010

First Edition

Library of Congress Cataloging-in-Publication Data

Wilson, Antoine.
You and a death in your family / by Antoine Wilson. — 1st ed.
p. cm. — (Family matters)
Includes bibliographical references and index.
ISBN 0-8239-3355-5
1. Grief in adolescence--Juvenile literature. 2. Bereavement in adolescence — Juvenile literature. 3. Loss (Psychology) in adolescence — Juvenile literature. 4. Teenagers and death — Juvenile literature. [1. Grief. 2. Death. 3. Loss (Psychology)] I. Title. II. Family matters (New York, N.Y.)
BF724.3.G73 W55 2000
155.9'37--dc21

00-011986

Manufactured in the United States of America

Contents

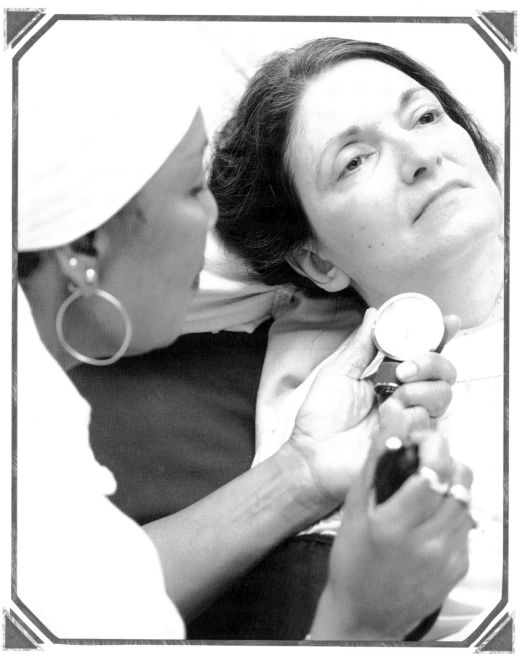

Coping with the death of a family member may be more difficult in the present day than ever before, since we are confronted with death less often than people were in the past.

Introduction

E ventually, everyone dies. We don't like to think about it because, deep down, we don't believe we're going to die. When someone close to us dies, we are suddenly reminded of the presence of death in our lives.

Modern medicine and modern living conditions have made death less visible than it was a hundred years ago. We might see death on television or in the movies, but we know that these deaths aren't real, so they do not affect us deeply. A hundred years ago, people were more familiar with death. If someone died of old age or of a disease like cancer, he or she often died at home, surrounded by family members. Today, people dying of cancer often die in hospitals, surrounded by doctors, nurses, and machines.

Death is something many people are uncomfortable talking about. As a result, we've forgotten how to cope with death. When a family member dies, we are often confused by how we feel. We don't know if what we're feeling is normal. And we have trouble talking to other people about our emotions.

When someone dies, we can't do anything to bring that person back. This idea is hard to accept. We who have been left behind must do something for ourselves to deal with the absence of this person in our lives. And we must learn how to support each other during this time of need.

The following chapters will help you understand what you're feeling and will help you cope with this tough situation.

Talking About Death

When someone in your family dies, it is important for you to talk about your feelings with someone else. Communicating your feelings openly can help you during the grieving process. Keeping all of your feelings bottled up inside won't help you cope with the loss of a loved one. Let your family know that you are willing to talk about your feelings.

THE IMPORTANCE OF COMMUNICATION

Is your family willing to talk about death? Sometimes parents and other adults will try to make death seem more pleasant by saying things like "she has passed on" or "he has gone on a long trip." They use these phrases to protect you from the reality of what has happened. If you feel that you can handle it, let your parents or other relatives know that you are willing to talk openly about death.

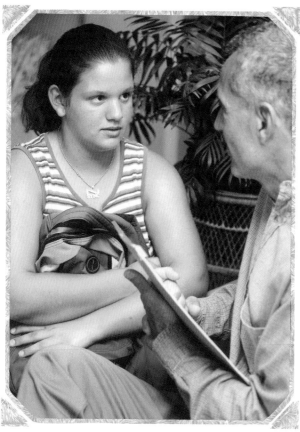
It is important to talk about a death in your family. A counselor can help you during the grieving process.

You may feel more comfortable talking to friends. This is fine. Often, young people are more willing to share their feelings when talking to other young people. However, your friends probably haven't had much experience coping with death. While they may provide a sympathetic ear, they might not know what to say. In any case, talking to friends can be a good way of sorting out what you're feeling. You can then share some of these talks with your family.

Whom Do I Talk To?

If you are not comfortable talking about death and your feelings with your friends or parents, you may want to talk to a counselor at some point. Counselors have special training and can help you during the grieving process. Also, it might be easier to voice your doubts to a counselor, since he or she is not also grieving. For example, you might feel uncomfortable about the fact that you didn't cry at the funeral, but you don't want to talk to your family about it because you don't want to make them feel bad. A counselor can help you come to terms with your feelings and behavior.

Speaking with a spiritual advisor, such as a priest, pastor, or rabbi, may help you with some of the big questions, like "Why did this have to happen?" or "What comes after death?" Whether or not you belong to a religion or believe in a particular faith, spiritual advisors can provide comfort and wise counsel. They are experts in the eternal cycle of birth and death.

2 Am I Feeling the Right Things?

Miguel and his older brother Pedro were very close. Pedro stuck up for Miguel at school and helped him make friends. When his brother died, Miguel was devastated. At the funeral, everyone was crying, but Miguel didn't feel like crying. He felt like he was watching everything from a distance.

Everyone reacts differently to the death of a family member. The shock of losing someone forever causes great sadness. But other feelings arise, too, and they can be confusing. Miguel, for example, felt sad but found himself unable to cry at his brother's funeral. This worried him. He wondered if his feelings were abnormal. Wasn't he supposed to cry at his brother's funeral?

When someone close to you dies, you will go through a range of emotions. You will feel different things at different times. You may not feel sad the whole time. You may find yourself reacting oddly, with anger or with laughter. It is important to let yourself feel however you feel and to express your emotions honestly. In other words, if you try to put on a happy face for everyone or try to cry when you don't feel like crying, you will keep yourself from going through the natural process of grieving.

Some doctors, like Elisabeth Kübler-Ross, have studied how we cope with death and have written about the range of emotions people go through when facing death. Not everyone feels all of these things, but most people experience grief in stages. Let yourself grieve at your own pace. Sometimes, when people try to rush themselves back to normal or keep their feelings bottled up inside, they can feel guilty or angry for years.

EMOTIONAL STAGES OF GRIEVING

Not everyone experiences the following reactions in this order. However, you might find yourself, or your family members, experiencing the following reactions to the death of a loved one.

Denial

Your first reaction to a sudden death might be: "It can't be true! I just saw him yesterday and he was fine." You may convince yourself that you're going to see this person again. This is called denial—when you refuse to accept the

Denial—refusal to accept the truth of a situation—is often one of the first stages of grieving.

truth of a situation. Very ill patients, when they are told that they will probably die from their illness, often go through a stage of denial. They act as if they are not very ill, or not ill at all. They talk about what they're going to do when they leave the hospital. A mother whose son has died might find herself still waiting for him to come home from school.

To an outsider, denial might seem silly, even counterproductive. We may want to try to bring the person to his or her senses, to force the truth on the person. This is not a good idea. Denial is a normal reaction. It acts as a protective shield against unexpected or tragic events. Denial gives us time to adjust to bad news. Do not be ashamed or embarrassed to go through a period of denial after learning about the death of a loved one. You're not losing your grip on reality. You're just giving yourself time to adjust.

Numbness and Confusion

Numbness and confusion can also be early reactions to the death of a family member. Like denial, these reactions can come right after hearing that someone has died. Numbness is when you don't feel anything—when you feel detached from the world around you. Confusion comes when you seem to feel everything at once.

Both numbness and confusion are reactions to feeling overwhelmed. Numbness, like denial, can help us find enough emotional distance to begin to cope with our loss. If you feel numb or detached, don't try to force your feelings. They will come eventually, when your mind is more prepared to deal with them.

The best way to cope with emotional confusion is to talk to someone about what you're feeling. Don't be afraid to cry. Crying lets emotions out and can actually make you feel less confused. Holding in your feelings can leave you feeling very lonely. When someone close to us dies, we often feel isolated and alone, even if we're surrounded by others who love us and offer us support. Try your best to reach out to others so that you won't be alone with your pain.

Anger

After denial, numbness, and confusion, the reality of the death begins to sink in. Often, the first reaction to this is anger and frustration. We feel powerless against death and lash out against those who we think hold power, such as doctors, hospitals, and God.

When something bad happens, human beings naturally try to blame someone or something. Sometimes, this blaming process is appropriate. For example, we blame a murderer for killing someone. At other times, we may end up blaming people who are innocent of any wrongdoing. For example, we might blame hospital nurses for the death of a sick relative. It's okay to express your anger and frustration. But if you blow up at someone who doesn't deserve it, apologize after you've cooled down. Let the person know that you're going through a difficult time. Also, if some of your family members blow up at little things, try to understand that their anger may stem from their sadness or confusion.

Bargaining

When a family member is dying, we might try to make a deal with God to spare that person's life. For example, we might say to ourselves, "If he makes it through this surgery, I'll try harder in school" or "If she gets better, I'll devote my life to helping others." Usually, we don't share these bargains with others. An extreme form of bargaining for the life of a loved one is when we say, "Take me instead, and let her live"—offering our lives in exchange.

These imaginary bargains are another reaction to our powerlessness against death. It is an attempt to gain some control over something we don't want to have happen. Though this type of bargaining is irrational, it is an important step in getting ready to say good-bye.

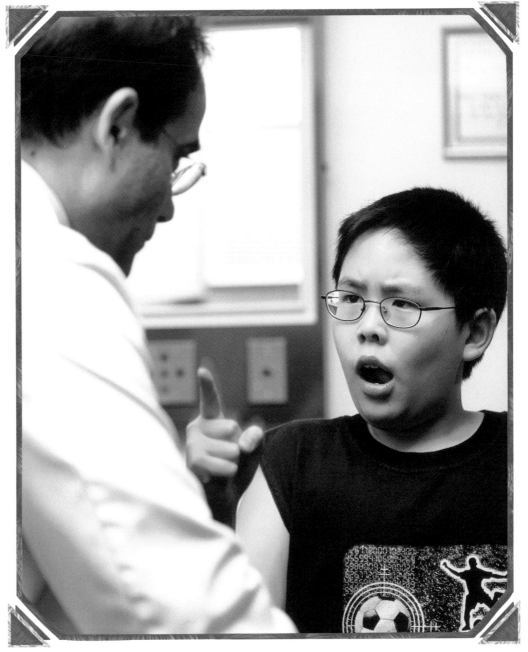

Anger at a loved one's death can stem from sadness or confusion.

Depression is a normal stage of mourning, but if you feel you've been depressed for too long, you should seek help.

Guilt and Regret

When a family member dies, we might be left with guilty feelings: "Why did I live, when he had to die?" We might feel guilty about an argument we had with the deceased. We might feel regret that we didn't show more affection when he or she was still alive. Guilt and regret are normal parts of the grieving process. Communicating with your family about your guilt and regret will help you get these things off your chest. If you keep your guilt and regret to yourself, they will not just disappear.

Depression

Depression is when nothing seems worth doing. As a normal stage of mourning, depression should not be ignored or rushed. However, if you find yourself heading deeper and deeper into depression, or if you feel that you've been depressed for too long, you should seek help. Talk to family members and/or seek counseling. Eventually, as your depression falls away, piece by piece, you will begin to resume the routines of daily life, and your mood should improve.

Acceptance

After you have come to terms with your loss, you will feel like yourself again. You might have sad moments, but you'll be able to function more normally. Don't try to force yourself into this state of acceptance. Acceptance will come naturally, eventually. Time is the great healer.

When a dying person has accepted the possibility of his or her own death, he or she might wish to see fewer people, or even be alone. You should understand that this is a natural reaction to the situation. It does not mean that the dying person has rejected you or your family members.

EMOTIONS AND YOUR FAMILY

After a death in your family, you might find yourself feeling one of two things: "Leave me alone!" or "Hey, what about me?" If your family is spending a lot of time together, you might feel like being alone for a while. However, too much isolation is not a good thing. A family in mourning can be like a band in which everyone is playing a different song. Only by making a special effort to communicate can everyone understand each other. Family members will often deal with death in different

If your family is spending a lot of time together, you might feel like being alone for a while.

ways at different times. Be sensitive to how your family feels, and listen to what they are saying about their feelings. Express your feelings as clearly and honestly as you can.

Respecting the Needs of Your Family

Families can contain a lot of different personalities. You might have a brother who likes to show off or a sister who likes to boss everyone around. One of your parents might be open about his or her emotions, while the other tends to keep things inside. Your mother might be in denial, while your father may be feeling a great deal of anger. You might feel isolated and confused, while your sister is busy trying to take care of everyone else. Respect how everyone is feeling and don't try to force them to feel something else.

Spending time together as a family is important. Whether you are talking, sharing memories, or simply sitting together and crying, you are helping each other cope with your loss.

3 When Parents, Grandparents, and Siblings Die

*C*armen's grandmother always took her side when Carmen and her parents got into arguments. Nona always brought Carmen gifts when she came over. Sometimes Carmen felt closer to her grandmother than she did to her mother or father. When Nona died, Carmen felt like she had lost the only person who could understand her. She felt alone and depressed.

Willy's grandfather was ill for a long time. He had been living with Willy and his family for over a year when he finally died. When Willy came home from school, his mother was crying. She told him that his grandfather had died. The first thing Willy felt was relief. The house wouldn't smell funny anymore, and he wouldn't have to help take care of his *grandfather. Then Willy saw his mother's tears and he felt guilty. He tried to feel sad, but he couldn't.*

When a Grandparent Dies

The death of a grandparent might be your first experience with the death of another human being. Sometimes grandparents die after a long illness, and sometimes they die unexpectedly. Your reaction to the death of a grandparent will probably depend on how close your relationship was.

Carmen's grandmother had played an important role in the balance of their family, and her death left a large gap in Carmen's life. Carmen had to learn how to connect with her parents in a new way. By sharing her feelings with her parents, and helping them to understand what her grandmother meant to her, Carmen developed a closer relationship with her parents.

Willy's situation was different. For him, his grandfather was a burden. Still, he had to

Your reaction to a grandparent's death will probably depend on how close your relationship was.

be sensitive to his mother's feelings. After all, she had just lost her father. Rather than trying to imitate his mother's grief, Willy was able to comfort his mother by encouraging her to talk about her favorite memories of her father.

WHEN A PARENT DIES

When Angie's mother died of lung cancer, Angie remembered all of the times she had hidden her mother's cigarettes. Now that her mother was gone, she kept thinking that she hadn't done enough to keep her mother from smoking. Even though everyone said that she shouldn't blame herself, she couldn't shake the feeling that she should have done more.

Raul's father died two months before Raul became the youngest-ever winner of a citywide chess tournament. Focusing on chess helped him cope with his father's absence. After he won, though, Raul felt cheated that his father wasn't there to recognize his achievement.

When Elizabeth's mother died, her father changed. He tried to put on a happy face for her, but she could see how badly he was hurting inside. He lost interest in his work and spent much of his time in front of the television, looking dazed. Elizabeth did the grocery shopping and the housework. She missed her mother, too, but she wanted to help her father get back to normal.

The death of a parent is one of the most painful and difficult moments in anyone's life. It can bring about many different feelings, some of which can place extra stress on you and your family. When your mother or father dies, your family probably will be thrown into confusion for a period of time. The most important thing the surviving family members can do is communicate—talking or even crying with each other.

Like Angie, many people feel guilty after the death of a loved one. Usually, these feelings are irrational—they don't make any logical sense. But they are an important stage in the grieving process. By talking to her father and brother about these feelings, Angie found out that they, too, had felt similar guilt. This helped her feel less isolated, and she was able to realize that she wasn't responsible for her mother's death.

Raul's frustration at having lost his father

The death of a parent can create stress and confusion for you and your family.

came from a deep anger at the unfairness of the world. "Why my father?" Raul asked. "Why now?" He looked around at all of the other boys who still had their fathers, and he felt cheated. It wasn't enough for his mother to be proud of him. She was always proud of him. He wanted to impress his father, who had always seemed distant. Raul expressed his feelings to his mother, and together they talked to a counselor. Eventually, Raul came to understand what lay behind his frustration and found a way to feel pride in his own achievements.

After her mother died, Elizabeth immediately took on the role of caretaker. She set aside her own feelings to make sure that the people around her were okay. She felt like she was doing a noble thing and that she was being a good, strong girl. Inside, though, Elizabeth was hurting. She distracted herself from her feelings by working harder. Eventually, she became very depressed and "broke down"—she didn't feel like she had energy for anything. She and her father talked to their pastor. He helped them see that she had avoided grieving for her mother by working so hard to take care of those around her. She finally began to mourn her mother's death, instead of trying to replace her mother.

WHEN YOUR BROTHER OR SISTER DIES

One day after school, Ronald and his brother had a big fight. Ronald's brother was older and had his driver's license, but he wouldn't drive Ronald to the mall. Ronald's brother wanted to hang out with his own friends. During their fight, Ronald said many mean things to his brother, and his brother left the house angry. That night, his brother was killed in a car accident. Ronald felt frustrated that he couldn't take back the mean things he had said. He also wondered if the accident would have happened if he and his brother hadn't fought.

Cathy's little sister was born with a heart condition and had to have many operations. She lived for three months and never got to come home from the hospital. Cathy's parents reacted to her sister's death in very different ways. Her father didn't want to talk about it. He spent longer hours at work. Her mother spent a lot of time in the room they had prepared for Cathy's sister. Cathy's parents started arguing a lot. Cathy was sad that her little sister had died, but she felt even more worried about her parents.

Ken's little brother got leukemia and had to go to the hospital for chemotherapy treatments. His hair fell out, and, despite the treatments, he seemed to be getting worse. Ken asked his parents if his brother was going to die. They said that he would probably be fine. Two weeks later, Ken's brother died. Ken

The death of a child can result in stress and communication problems for parents and siblings. It may seem unfair that a young person has died.

was confused. Why didn't his parents tell him that his brother was going to die?

The death of a sibling (brother or sister) can have a powerful impact on a family. When someone dies young, it results in a heightened sense of anger and frustration in the survivors. The world seems unfair: Young people, we think, aren't supposed to die. When there is a lot of anger and frustration in a family, blame gets thrown around a lot more.

Communicate, Communicate, Communicate

Your parents may have difficulty communicating their feelings, even with each other. You might hear that there is a very high divorce rate in families that have lost a child. This is a myth, or a piece of information that gets spread around but isn't true. The most important things are to keep the channels of communication open and to speak honestly about what you're feeling. Different family members will react differently at different times. Some, including you, might not feel like talking about the death. Be patient with your family and with yourself.

Your reaction to the death of a brother or sister will change over time. While you will probably have some of the emotional reactions outlined earlier in this book, more complicated emotions will arise, depending on the type of relationship you had with your brother or sister.

Ronald's Family: Remember the Good and the Bad

Ronald's situation is one of the most difficult to deal with. He didn't get a chance to take back any of the mean things that he said to his brother. This left him feeling very guilty after his brother's death.

Ronald discussed this with his parents and found some ways to accept the fact that he could never speak to his brother again. His mother reminded him of all the nice things he had done for his brother, and that his brother knew Ronald loved him. Ronald also wrote a letter to his brother, apologizing for what he had said, and this letter was buried with Ronald. Ronald's father reminded him that we are bound to have disagreements now and then, and that we never know when someone we love will be taken from us. In this way, Ronald came to understand that the argument he had with his brother was a small event, when looked at in the context of his entire relationship with his brother.

Cathy's Family: Isolation and Blame

Family problems did arise after Cathy's sister died. Her parents isolated themselves and stopped communicating. Cathy didn't know what to do. She decided to approach her parents one at a time and try to talk about her sister's death. Eventually, she was able to get her parents in the same room, and the three of them talked about how they felt. Both her mother and father confessed to blaming themselves for her sister's death. When her parents understood that, in their isolation, they had been feeling the same thing, they felt relieved, and it became easier for Cathy to tell them how she was feeling, too

Ken's Family: Truth and Anger

Ken's parents tried to hide the seriousness of his brother's illness from him. His brother's death came as a shock to Ken, but his parents had been preparing themselves the whole time. Ken felt angry that his parents had hidden the facts from him. He talked to a counselor who agreed that his parents should have told him what was going on.

The counselor encouraged Ken to think about why his parents had decided to hide the truth from him. Ken spoke to his parents about it. They told him that they didn't want to scare him. He told them about how unprepared he was for his brother's death and how angry he was. His parents admitted that they should have told him sooner. Ken understood that his parents loved him and that they had tried to protect him. His parents understood that they had made a mistake in not being frank with him about what was happening.

SUICIDE OR VIOLENT DEATH

Jamie was the school mascot. He dressed up in a bear suit at all the games and did cartwheels and flips. He was also the class clown. Everyone loved being around Jamie. He was funny and had lots of energy. Then, one day, he killed himself. The whole school was in shock. Nobody could understand it. Jamie's sister

Suicide and violent death can be especially hard to cope with.

blamed herself for not noticing any warning signs. She told herself that she could have prevented her brother's suicide if only she had paid more attention to him.

Ryan's father was shot and killed in a grocery store parking lot by someone who wanted to steal his car. The would-be thief panicked and left the car behind. He was never caught. Ryan's life changed completely after that. He had a lot of feelings he couldn't express, but mostly he felt angry. He got into fights at school and couldn't concentrate on studying. Why his father? It didn't make any sense.

Suicide and violent death can be extremely hard to cope with, especially when they happen in our immediate family. When someone dies of a disease, we might ask "Why?" but we will eventually understand the role disease plays in the cycle of life and death. When someone dies in a car accident, we might be shocked by the suddenness of the death, and by the tragedy of it, but we understand that car accidents are a part of modern life. However, when someone is murdered, or takes his or her own life, understanding his or her death can be much more difficult, even impossible.

Where to Put the Blame?

A normal reaction to suicide is to blame ourselves. We scour our memories, searching for what we might have done to prevent this senseless death. Jamie's sister blamed herself for not noticing any warning signs. But Jamie didn't show any warning signs. He seemed happy

Suicide—It's Not a Joke

If someone close to you talks to you about committing suicide, don't assume that he or she is joking. People rarely make that kind of joke unless they have considered killing themselves. If someone tells you that he or she is thinking of suicide, it might be a call for help. Talk to your parents and/or a counselor about how to get your friend some help.

with life. He hid his feelings behind a mask of happiness, and perhaps he felt isolated in his pain. No one will ever know exactly how he felt. Coping with the suicide of someone close to you will take time, but eventually your life will return to near-normal. The question "Why?" will probably remain with you for the rest of your life because it is a question that cannot be answered.

Violent death is especially hard to cope with for one reason. People aren't supposed to kill other people. But they do. And often, they kill people they don't know, for stupid reasons. When those people are people we know, we are left with many questions and few answers. The man who killed Ryan's father killed him because he wanted to steal his car. In the end, the killer never even took the car. Ryan's father was killed for no reason at all. And, since his father's murderer was never caught, Ryan had no one to blame. This is an extremely difficult idea to accept. In a situation like this, it might be best for the surviving family to seek the help of a counselor or pastor.

When a Pet Dies

*F*reida's golden retriever, Atlas, was a good friend. Atlas liked to wait for Freida to come home from school, and he always slept at the foot of Freida's bed. Then Atlas got sick. Instead of leaping up to greet Freida after school, he just lay there, yawning and crying. Freida and her mother took Atlas to the animal doctor, who told them Atlas was very ill and should be put to sleep. Freida didn't want Atlas to die, but she didn't want Atlas to suffer anymore either. After they put Atlas to sleep, they had him cremated and kept his ashes in a special urn in the house.

The loss of a pet can be a young person's first introduction to death. Pets, especially those we consider our friends, can play an active and important role in our families. When a pet dies, he or she can

The death of a pet may be your first experience with death. You should allow yourself to grieve for your loss. Then, you may be able to welcome a new pet into your life.

leave an empty place in our lives. After the death of a pet, try to respect the feelings of your family members. Even if you were not very close to the pet, others in your family might be feeling a great deal of pain. If you were close to the pet, you might find yourself thinking, "Why am I so sad? He was only a pet." Respect your own feelings. Don't hide your sadness. You have experienced a real loss, and you should be allowed to grieve.

SAYING GOOD-BYE TO YOUR PET

Sometimes, when a pet is very ill or has been badly hurt, the veterinarian (pet doctor) will suggest that he or she be "put to sleep" or "put down." Deciding to put a pet to sleep can be very difficult, but it can shorten the pet's suffering. It also gives you a chance to say good-bye.

You can, as a family, do something to honor your pet's memory. Give your pet a funeral and share memories. Bury your pet with his or her favorite toys. Some people bury their pets in their backyards. This may or may not be legal in your neighborhood. Other people have their pets cremated and bury the ashes or keep them somewhere in the house.

Your parents may want to buy another pet immediately. If you feel that they're only trying to replace your old pet, let them know that you want to wait awhile, to give yourself a chance to say good-bye to the old pet. No pet will ever replace your old pet, though another can be welcomed into your family after you've had a chance to say good-bye.

5 The Funeral and After: Putting the Pieces Back Together

All societies perform some sort of ritual when someone dies. Funerals are a ritual in which loved ones can assemble and say good-bye to those who have died. They are also opportunities for sharing memories about our loved ones. Usually, funerals happen in a place of worship or in a funeral home. A funeral helps us to accept and recognize that our loved one has died. As a result, funerals are often emotional ceremonies.

Your family may not know whether you are ready to attend a funeral. If you feel like you do want to go, let them know. If you feel too sad to go to the funeral, try to help them understand how you feel. Not attending someone's funeral does not mean that you didn't love the person or aren't mourning his or her death in your own way. You should, if you can, attend the funeral. It will help you say good-bye to your loved one.

THE CEREMONY

Usually, the ceremony is led by a pastor or other religious person, or a funeral director. Often, organ music is played, and passages are read from the Bible or other religious texts. In many funerals, family members and close friends are given a chance to speak. If you think you want to speak at the funeral, ask beforehand. You might want to prepare something ahead of time, like a memory you would like to share, or a tribute.

Sometimes, funerals include a viewing. This gives you an opportunity to see the body of your loved one for the last time. Usually, the body has been prepared for viewing, with makeup and dressed in a favorite suit or dress. Don't expect the body to look exactly like the person you knew. Viewing the body can help you realize that the person you knew is gone, and that their spirit is elsewhere. Talk with your family about whether or not you want to participate in the viewing.

After the funeral, there may be a burial ceremony, in which the coffin or casket is laid into the earth at a cemetery. This can be very emotional as well because it is so final. Sometimes, bodies are cremated rather than buried. This means that they are burned and reduced to ash. The ashes of a loved one might then be buried, placed in a mausoleum, or scattered over a favorite place, like the ocean. Occasionally, people will donate their bodies to science, which means that their bodily organs will be

Writing a letter to a deceased loved one can help you express your grief.

used to help other people, contributing to others' lives even after death.

Talk to your family about the funeral ahead of time, and decide how much you want to involve yourself. The funeral is an important ritual that can make the grieving process easier to accept.

WORKING THROUGH YOUR GRIEF AND RETURNING TO LIFE

Besides the funeral, we can create our own rituals to help us in our grief. You may want to write a letter to your loved one, or make a collage or photo album to collect your memories. Or maybe you can edit family movies to make a tribute to your loved one. Doing this as a family can help us to communicate how we feel as we move into the later stages of grief, when it feels most important to keep the memory of a loved one alive.

Keep Active

Creative activities, such as writing poetry or drawing and painting, can help us explore ourselves and how we feel. And when they're shared with others, even if only our immediate family, we can communicate some of those deep feelings. You might want to keep a journal to help you understand what you're feeling. And, later in life, you might find yourself helping someone else who has lost someone close.

Dealing with School

Returning to school after a death in the family can be very difficult. At first you might find it difficult to concentrate in class. You'll probably have to make up some work and you'll still be working through your grief. It will take a little while to adjust. Talk to your teachers and let them know what's going on. They will understand that you are going through a lot.

You will want to decide how, if at all, you wish your classmates to learn about

You may have trouble concentrating in school after the death of a family member. Be sure to let your teachers know what has happened.

your loss. It can be embarrassing to have a teacher announce it to the class, so it is probably best just to tell your friends what happened. They may not know how to react. Some of your friends and classmates might avoid you, not because they don't like you anymore, but because they don't know how to act in this situation. They don't want to make you hurt even more. A small effort on your part to make them feel comfortable will go a long way.

After some time, you will enter a stage of acceptance, and your emotional pain will lessen. Some young people express a fear of forgetting their loved ones who have died. They worry that if they return to "life as usual," all traces of those who have died will be forgotten. But you can continue to live your life while also honoring those who have died. They can remain an inspiration to us throughout the rest of our lives. Their legacies can inspire us to do great things in their names. And the things they have taught us will remain with us forever.

Glossary

cancer   Disease in which abnormal cells grow uncontrolled, invading and destroying other parts of the body.

chemotherapy   Treatment for cancer that uses chemicals or drugs; can cause hair loss.

cremation   The process of burning a dead body and reducing it to ash.

denial   Refuse to accept the truth of a situation.

grieving   Feeling grief after someone has died.

irrational   Behaving in a way that is not clear.

isolation   Being alone or feeling alone.

leukemia   Cancer of white blood cells and white blood-producing cells.

mourning   Period of expressing grief or sorrow for someone who has died.

Where to Go for Help

IN THE UNITED STATES

Centering Corporation
1531 N. Saddle Creek Road
Omaha, NE 68104
(402) 553-1200
Web site: http://www.webhealing.com/centering

The Compassionate Friends, Inc.
P.O. Box 3696
Oak Brook, IL 60522-3696
(630) 990-0010
Web site: http://www.compassionatefriends.org/

Groww: Grief Recovery Online
931 N. State Road 434
Suite 1201-358

Altamonte Springs, FL 32714
Web site: http://www.groww.com/

The Kids' Place: A Grief Support Center for Children and
    Their Families
P.O. Box 258
Edmond, OK 73083
(405) 844-KIDS (5437)
Web site: http://www.kidsplace.org/

TAG: Teen Age Grief, Inc.
P.O. Box 220034
Newhall, CA 91322-0034
(661) 253-1932
Web site: http://www.smartlink.net/~tag/index.html

In Canada

Bereaved Families of Ontario
562 Eglinton Avenue East, Suite 401
Toronto, ON M4P 1P1
(416) 440-0290
Web site: http://www.inforamp.net/~bfo/index.html

The Childhood Cancer Foundation—Candlelighters Canada
55 Eglinton Avenue East, Suite 401
Toronto, ON M4P 1G8
(800) 363-1062 or (416) 489-6440
Web site: http://www.candlelighters.ca/

For Further Reading

Bode, Janet. *Death Is Hard to Live With: Teenagers Talk About How They Cope with Loss.* New York: Delacorte Press, 1993.

Grollman, Earl A. *Living When a Loved One Has Died.* Boston: Beacon Press, 1995.

Hickman, Martha Whitmore. *Healing After Loss: Daily Meditations for Working Through Grief.* New York: Avon Books, 1994.

Johnson, Marvin, and Joy Johnson. *Children Grieve, Too: Helping Children Cope with Grief.* Omaha, NE: Centering Corp., 1998.

Kübler-Ross, Elisabeth. *On Death and Dying.* New York: Scribner Classics, 1997.

Rofes, Eric E. *The Kids' Book About Death and Dying: By and for Kids.* Boston: Little, Brown, 1985.

Index

ABOUT THE AUTHOR

Antoine Wilson is a writer living in eastern Iowa.

PHOTO CREDITS

Cover and Interior Shots by Ira Fox

DESIGN

Geri Giordano

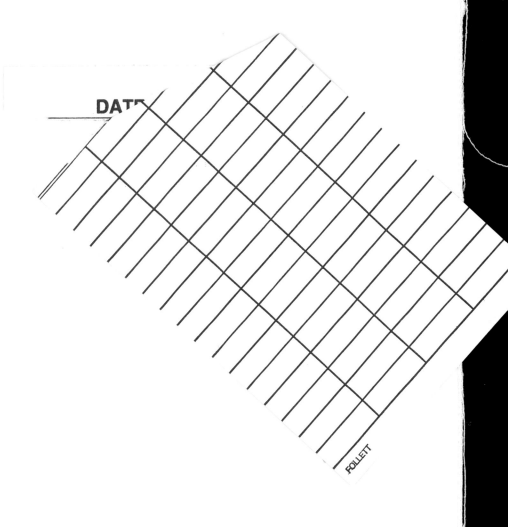

DATE

FOLLETT